Selected Duets

for CLARINET

Published in Two Volumes:

VOLUME I (Easy-Medium)

● **VOLUME II (Advanced)**

Compiled and Edited

by H. VOXMAN

RUBANK®

HAL•LEONARD®
CORPORATION

7777 W. BLUEMOUND RD. P.O. BOX 13819 MILWAUKEE, WI 53213

PREFACE

Duet playing affords the student the most intimate form of ensemble experience. The problems of technic, tone quality, intonation, and ensemble balance are brought into the sharpest relief. Careful attention must be given to style as indicated by the printed page and as demanded by the intangibles of good taste.

Among the several duets included in this volume, the most frequently occurring of the unfamiliar embellishments is the *appoggiatura* (long grace note). It is generally (but not always) played as written:

The performer must distinguish between the inverted mordent (⩘) and the mordent (⩘) :

In the music of Bach and Quantz, the trill in most instances should begin with the upper accessory.

H. Voxman

CONTENTS

DUET
Based Upon the Sonata in C, K.296

Mozart

Andante sostenuto

RONDO

Allegro

DUET
Based Upon the Sonata in E♭, K. 380

Mozart

RONDO
Allegro

DUET

Based Upon the Sonata in B♭, K. 454

Largo (in eight)

Mozart

Allegretto

Two Duets in Concert Style
DUET IN G MAJOR

Quantz

DUET IN C MAJOR

Allegro

Ferling

Six Duets Based Upon the Works of Bach
TWO-VOICED FUGUE

Bach

TWO-PART INVENTION NO. IV

Bach

TWO-PART INVENTION NO. VIII

Vivace (♩ = 120–126)

Bach

TWO-PART INVENTION NO. X

Bach

TWO-PART INVENTION NO.XV

Bach

LITTLE PRELUDE

Vivace (♩.=72)

Bach

DUET NO. 3

Based Upon the Duo in B♭ for Clarinet and Bassoon

Beethoven

Allegro sostenuto

Aria con Variazioni
Andantino con moto

Variation II

Variation III

Variation IV